TRAGEDY! TALES FROM THE TITANIC

A Deadly Journey

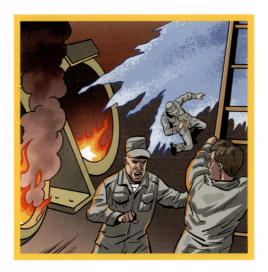

BY SARAH EASON
ILLUSTRATED BY KEVIN HOPGOOD

BEARPORT PUBLISHING

Minneapolis, Minnesota

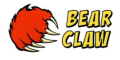

BEAR CLAW

Credits

20, © Shutterstock/Henk Vrieselaar; 21t, © Shutterstock/Muratart; 21b, © Wikimedia Commons/ J.W. Barker; 22t, © Wikimedia Commons; 22b, © Wikimedia Commons/New York Times; 23, © Wikimedia Commons/Francis Godolphin Osbourne Stuart.

Editor: Jennifer Sanderson
Proofreader: Katie Dicker
Designer: Paul Myerscough
Picture Researcher: Katie Dicker

Bearport Publishing Company Product Development Team

Publisher: Jen Jenson; Director of Product Development: Spencer Brinker; Managing Editor: Allison Juda; Editor: Cole Nelson; Associate Editor: Naomi Reich; Associate Editor: Tiana Tran; Art Director: Colin O'Dea; Designer: Kim Jones; Designer: Kayla Eggert; Product Development Specialist: Owen Hamlin

Statement on Usage of Generative Artificial Intelligence

Bearport Publishing remains committed to publishing high-quality nonfiction books. Therefore, we restrict the use of generative AI to ensure accuracy of all text and visual components pertaining to a book's subject. See BearportPublishing.com for details.

A Note on Graphic Narrative Nonfiction

This graphic story is a dramatization based on true events. It is intended to give the reader a sense of the narrative rather than a presentation of actual details as they occurred.

Library of Congress Cataloging-in-Publication Data

Names: Eason, Sarah, author. | Hopgood, Kevin, illustrator.
Title: A deadly journey / Sarah Eason ; Illustrated by Kevin Hopgood.
Description: Bear claw books. | Minneapolis, Minnesota : Bearport
  Publishing Company, 2025. | Series: Tragedy! Tales from the Titanic |
  Includes bibliographical references and index.
Identifiers: LCCN 2024034188 (print) | LCCN 2024034189 (ebook) | ISBN
  9798892328555 (library binding) | ISBN 9798892329453 (paperback) | ISBN
  9798892328623 (ebook)
Subjects: LCSH: Titanic (Steamship)--Juvenile literature. | Titanic
  (Steamship)--Comic books, strips, etc. | Ocean liners--Great
  Britain--History--20th century--Juvenile literature. | Ocean
  liners--Great Britain--History--20th century--Comic books, strips, etc.
  | Shipwrecks--North Atlantic Ocean--History--20th century--Juvenile
  literature. | Shipwrecks--North Atlantic Ocean--History--20th
  century--Comic books, strips, etc. | Graphic novels.
Classification: LCC G530.T6 E24 2025 (print) | LCC G530.T6 (ebook) | DDC
  910.9163/4--dc23/eng20240725
LC record available at https://lccn.loc.gov/2024034188
LC ebook record available at https://lccn.loc.gov/2024034189

For more information, write to Bearport Publishing, 5357 Penn Avenue South, Minneapolis, MN 55419.

Contents

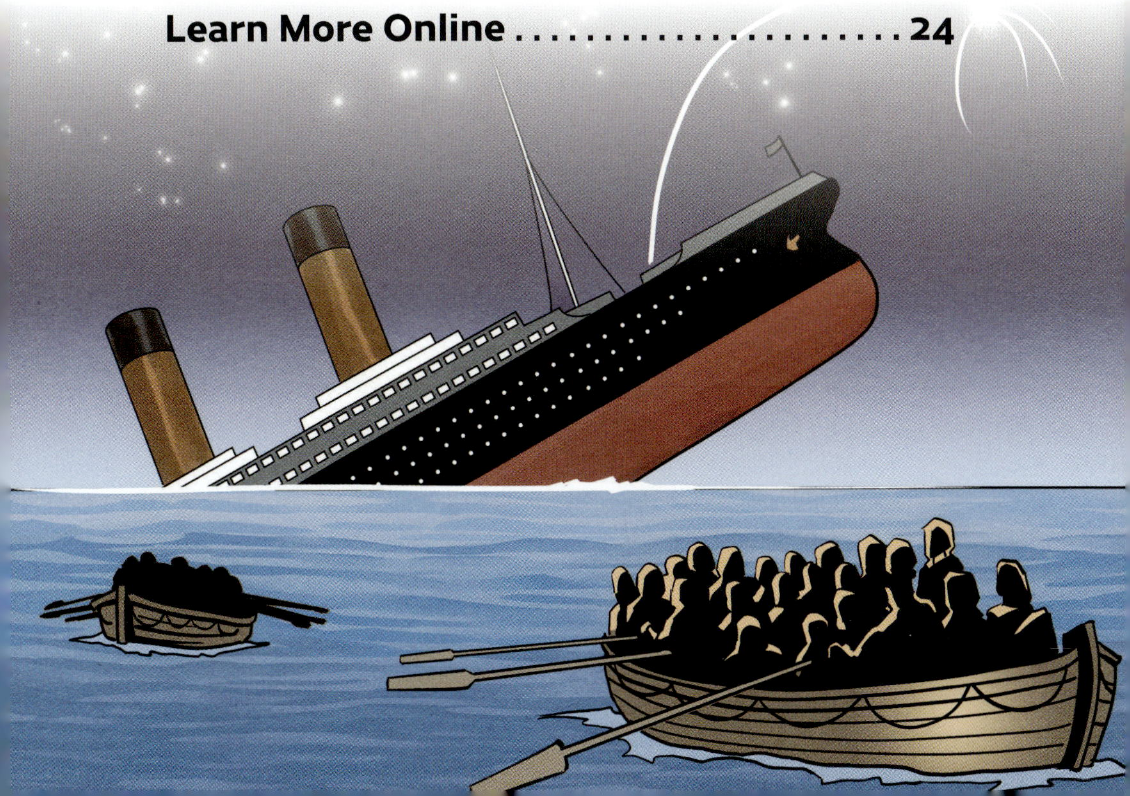

CHAPTER 1

Setting Sail

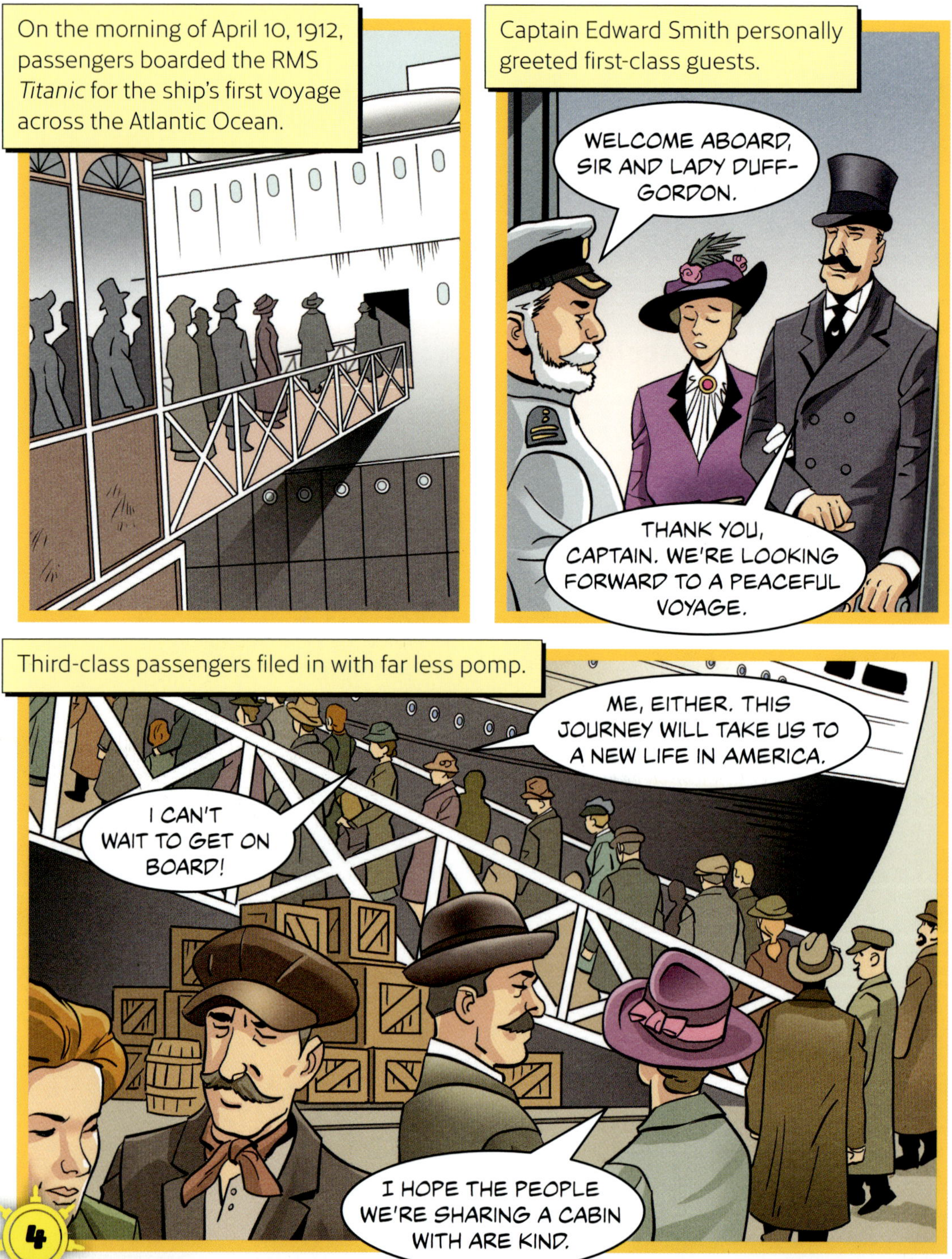
On the morning of April 10, 1912, passengers boarded the RMS *Titanic* for the ship's first voyage across the Atlantic Ocean.
Captain Edward Smith personally greeted first-class guests.
WELCOME ABOARD, SIR AND LADY DUFF-GORDON.
THANK YOU, CAPTAIN. WE'RE LOOKING FORWARD TO A PEACEFUL VOYAGE.
Third-class passengers filed in with far less pomp.
I CAN'T WAIT TO GET ON BOARD!
ME, EITHER. THIS JOURNEY WILL TAKE US TO A NEW LIFE IN AMERICA.
I HOPE THE PEOPLE WE'RE SHARING A CABIN WITH ARE KIND.

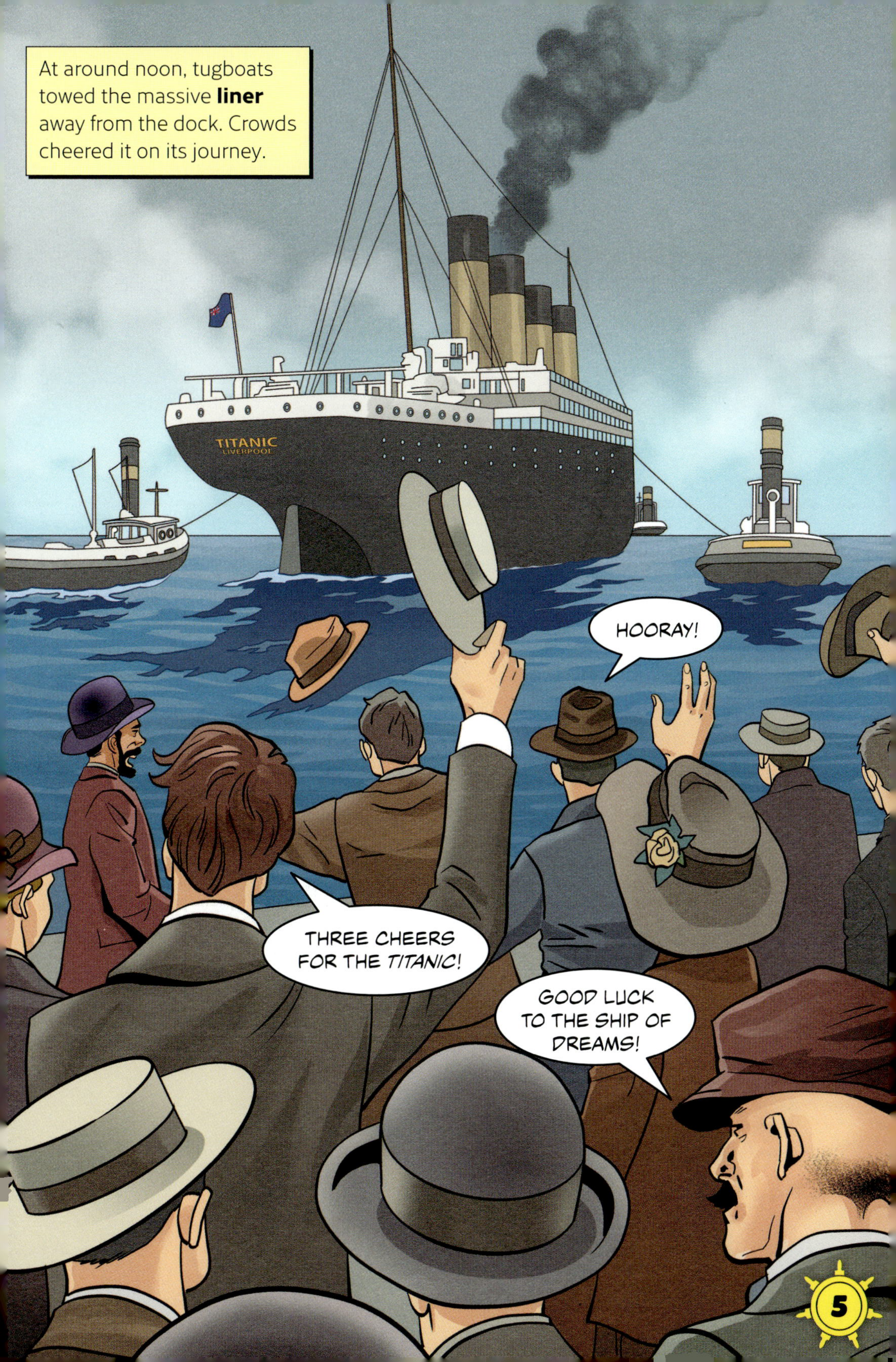
At around noon, tugboats towed the massive **liner** away from the dock. Crowds cheered it on its journey.
TITANIC LIVERPOOL
HOORAY!
THREE CHEERS FOR THE *TITANIC*!
GOOD LUCK TO THE SHIP OF DREAMS!

CHAPTER 2

A Floating Hotel

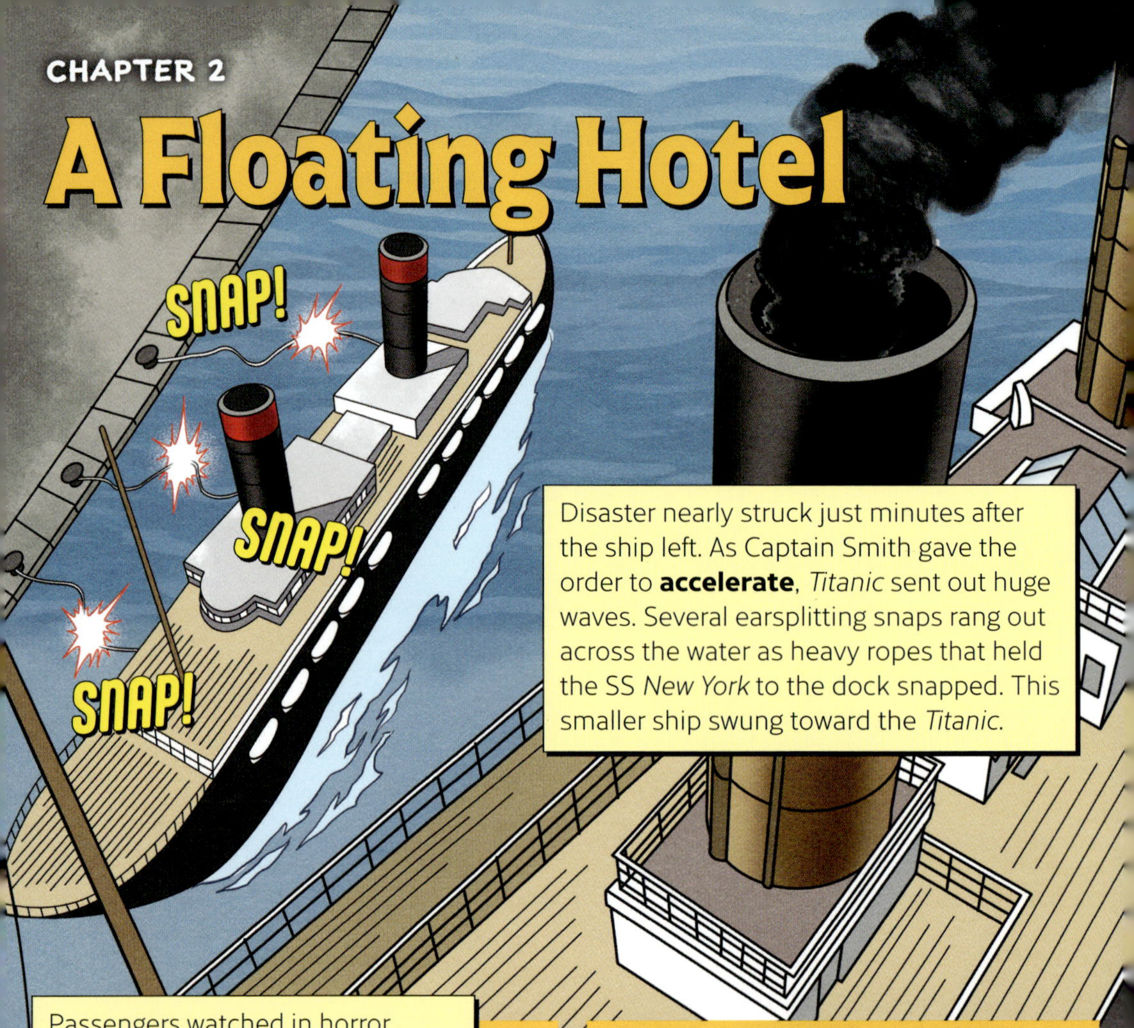
SNAP!
SNAP!
SNAP!
Disaster nearly struck just minutes after the ship left. As Captain Smith gave the order to **accelerate**, *Titanic* sent out huge waves. Several earsplitting snaps rang out across the water as heavy ropes that held the SS *New York* to the dock snapped. This smaller ship swung toward the *Titanic*.

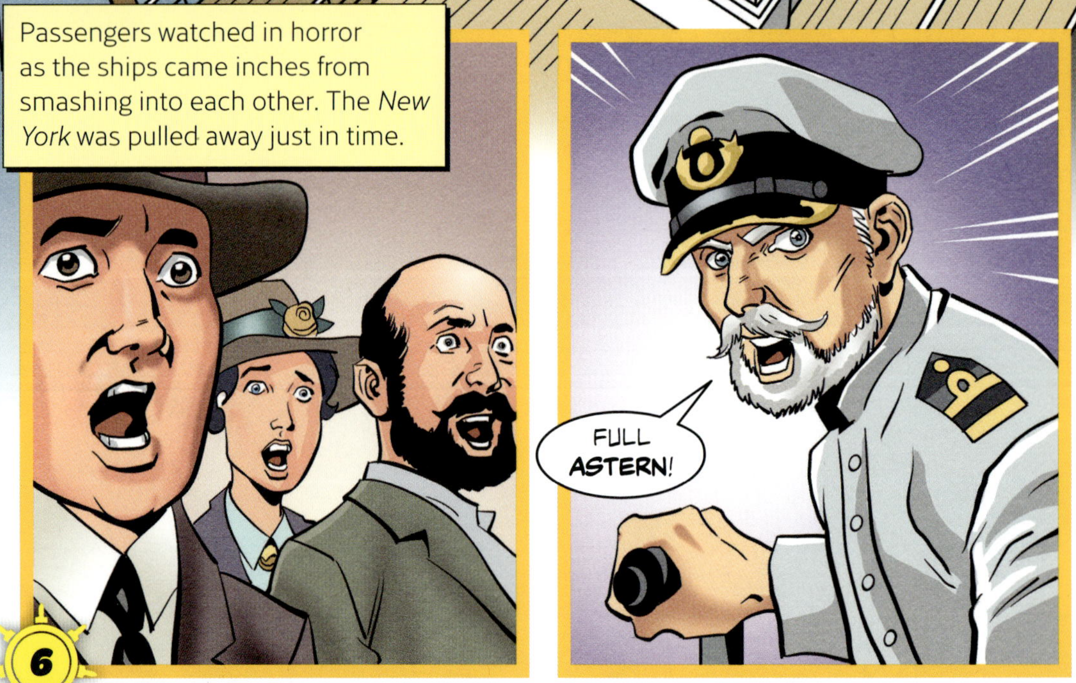
Passengers watched in horror as the ships came inches from smashing into each other. The *New York* was pulled away just in time.
FULL ASTERN!

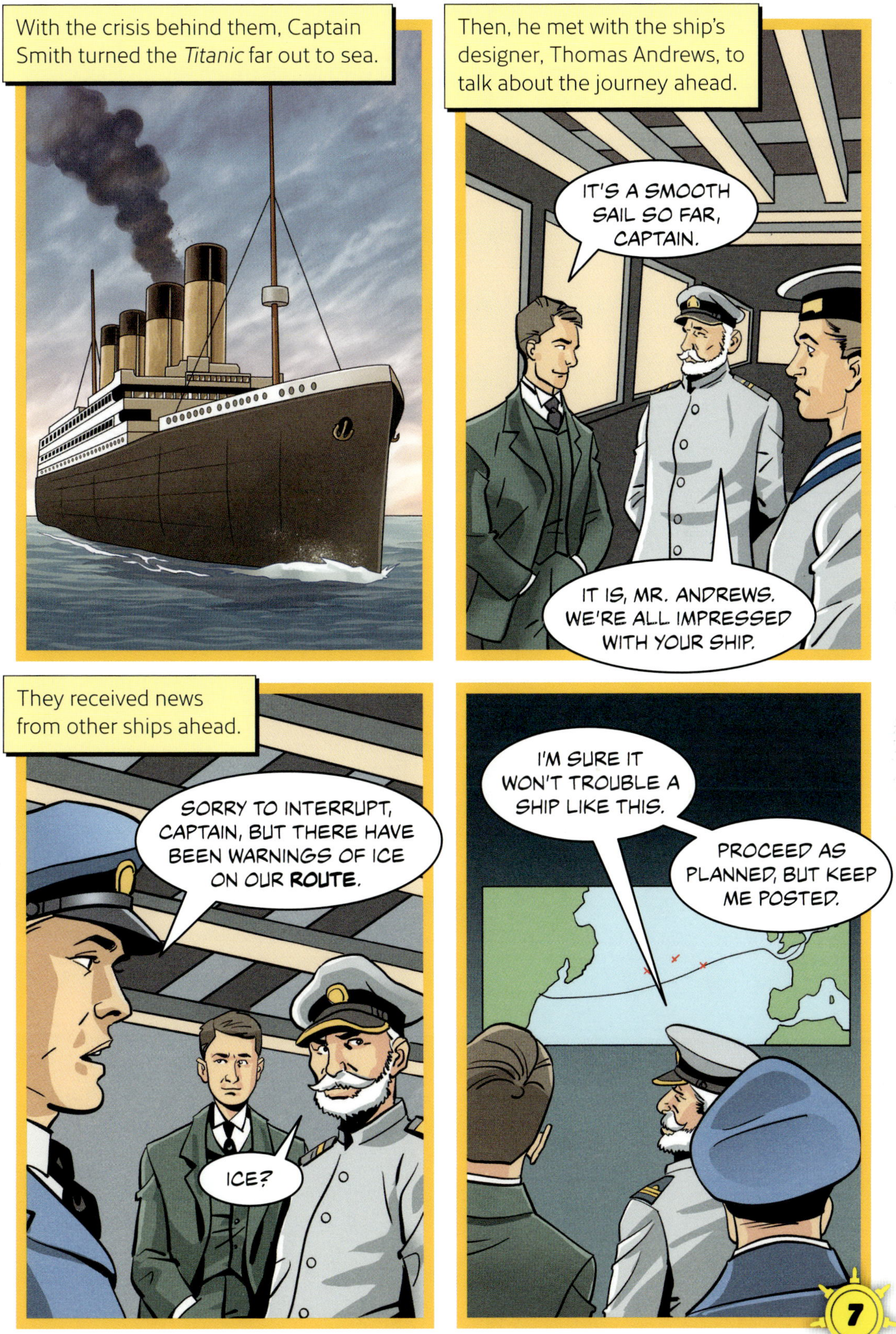
With the crisis behind them, Captain Smith turned the *Titanic* far out to sea.
Then, he met with the ship's designer, Thomas Andrews, to talk about the journey ahead.
IT'S A SMOOTH SAIL SO FAR, CAPTAIN.
IT IS, MR. ANDREWS. WE'RE ALL IMPRESSED WITH YOUR SHIP.
They received news from other ships ahead.
SORRY TO INTERRUPT, CAPTAIN, BUT THERE HAVE BEEN WARNINGS OF ICE ON OUR **ROUTE**.
ICE?
I'M SURE IT WON'T TROUBLE A SHIP LIKE THIS.
PROCEED AS PLANNED, BUT KEEP ME POSTED.

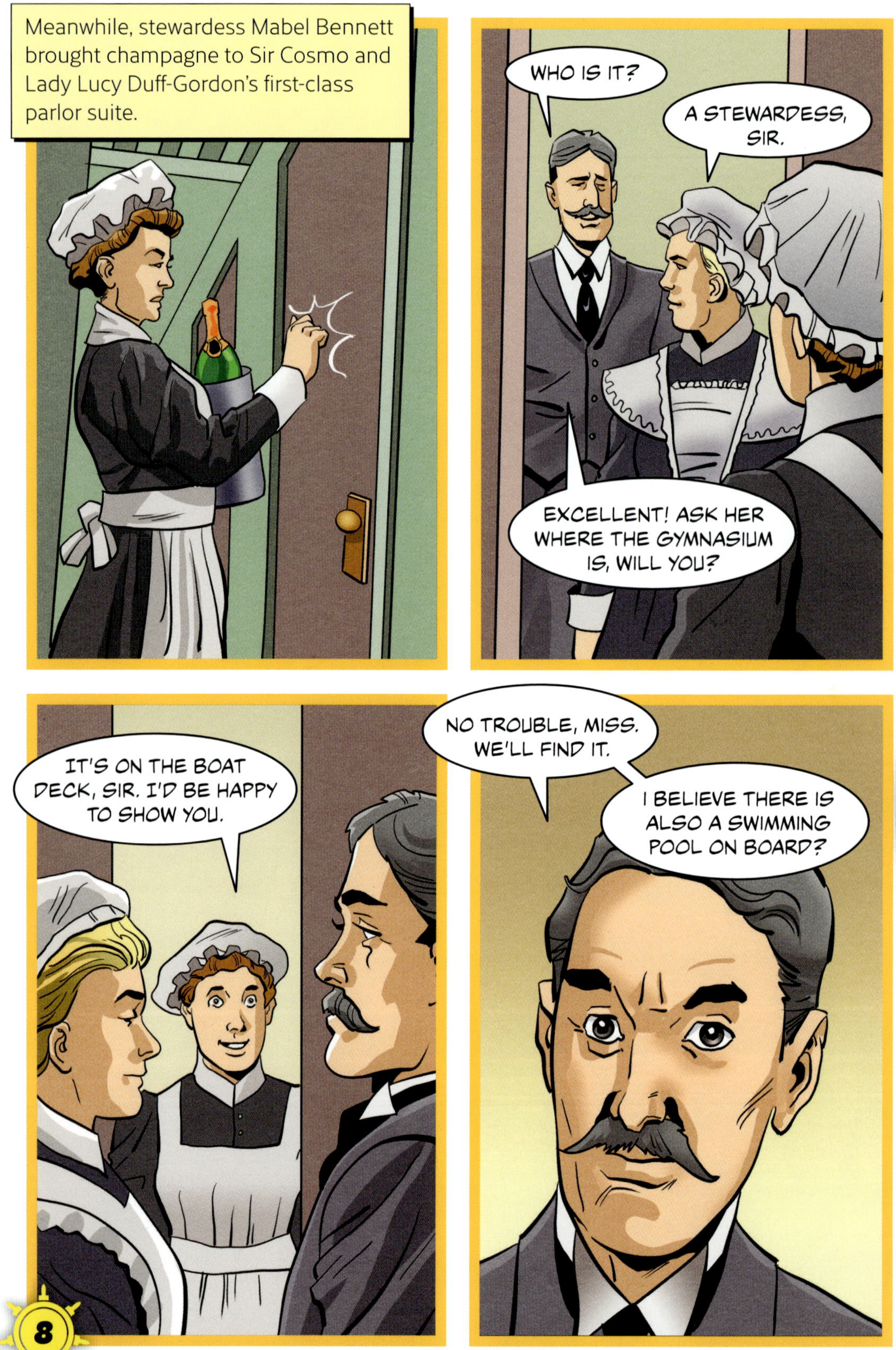
Meanwhile, stewardess Mabel Bennett brought champagne to Sir Cosmo and Lady Lucy Duff-Gordon's first-class parlor suite.
WHO IS IT?
A STEWARDESS, SIR.
EXCELLENT! ASK HER WHERE THE GYMNASIUM IS, WILL YOU?
IT'S ON THE BOAT DECK, SIR. I'D BE HAPPY TO SHOW YOU.
NO TROUBLE, MISS. WE'LL FIND IT.
I BELIEVE THERE IS ALSO A SWIMMING POOL ON BOARD?

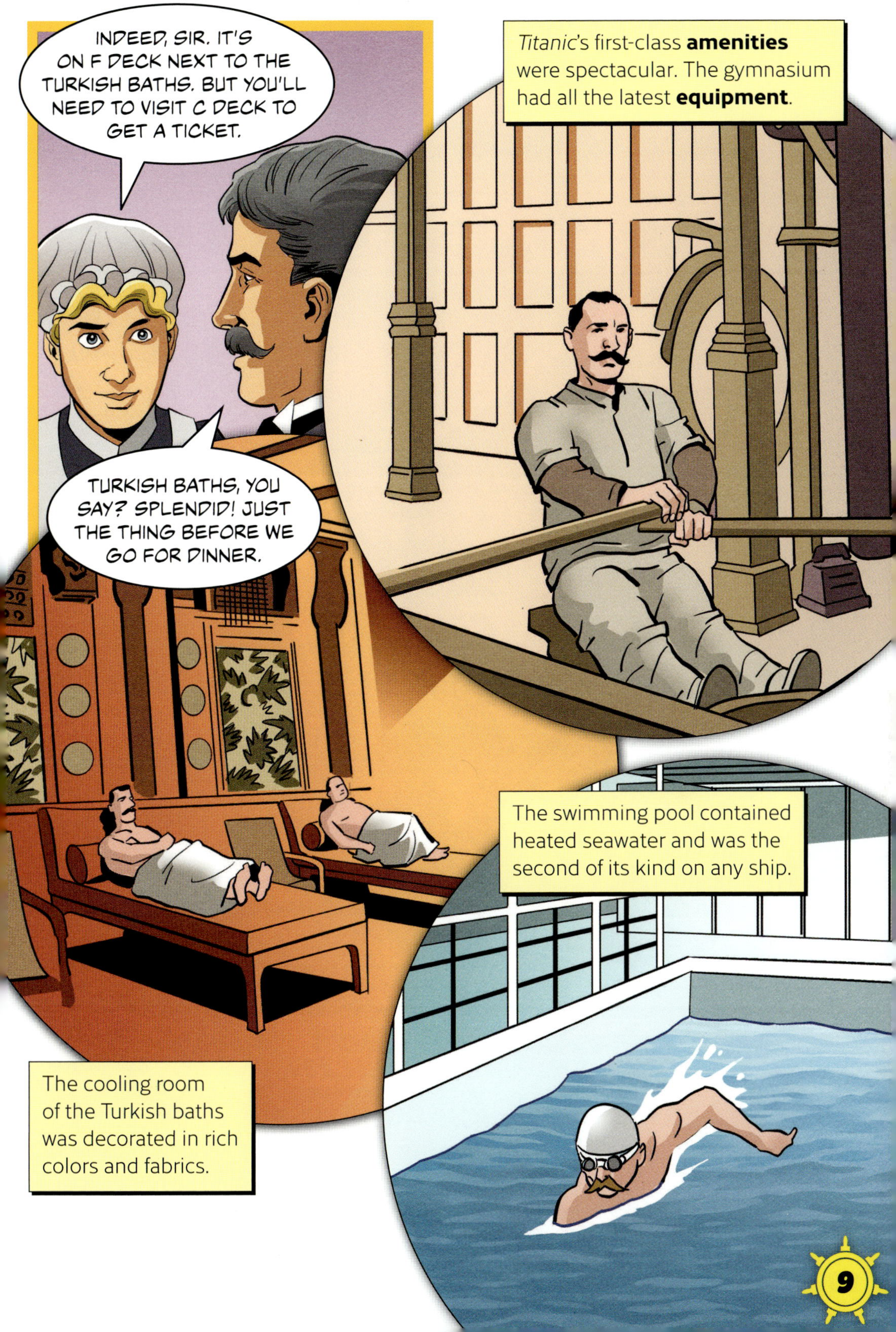
INDEED, SIR. IT'S ON F DECK NEXT TO THE TURKISH BATHS. BUT YOU'LL NEED TO VISIT C DECK TO GET A TICKET.
TURKISH BATHS, YOU SAY? SPLENDID! JUST THE THING BEFORE WE GO FOR DINNER.
Titanic's first-class **amenities** were spectacular. The gymnasium had all the latest **equipment**.
The cooling room of the Turkish baths was decorated in rich colors and fabrics.
The swimming pool contained heated seawater and was the second of its kind on any ship.

The *Titanic*'s **bugler** signaled dinnertime for first-class passengers, and guests made their way down the grand staircase to the dining rooms.

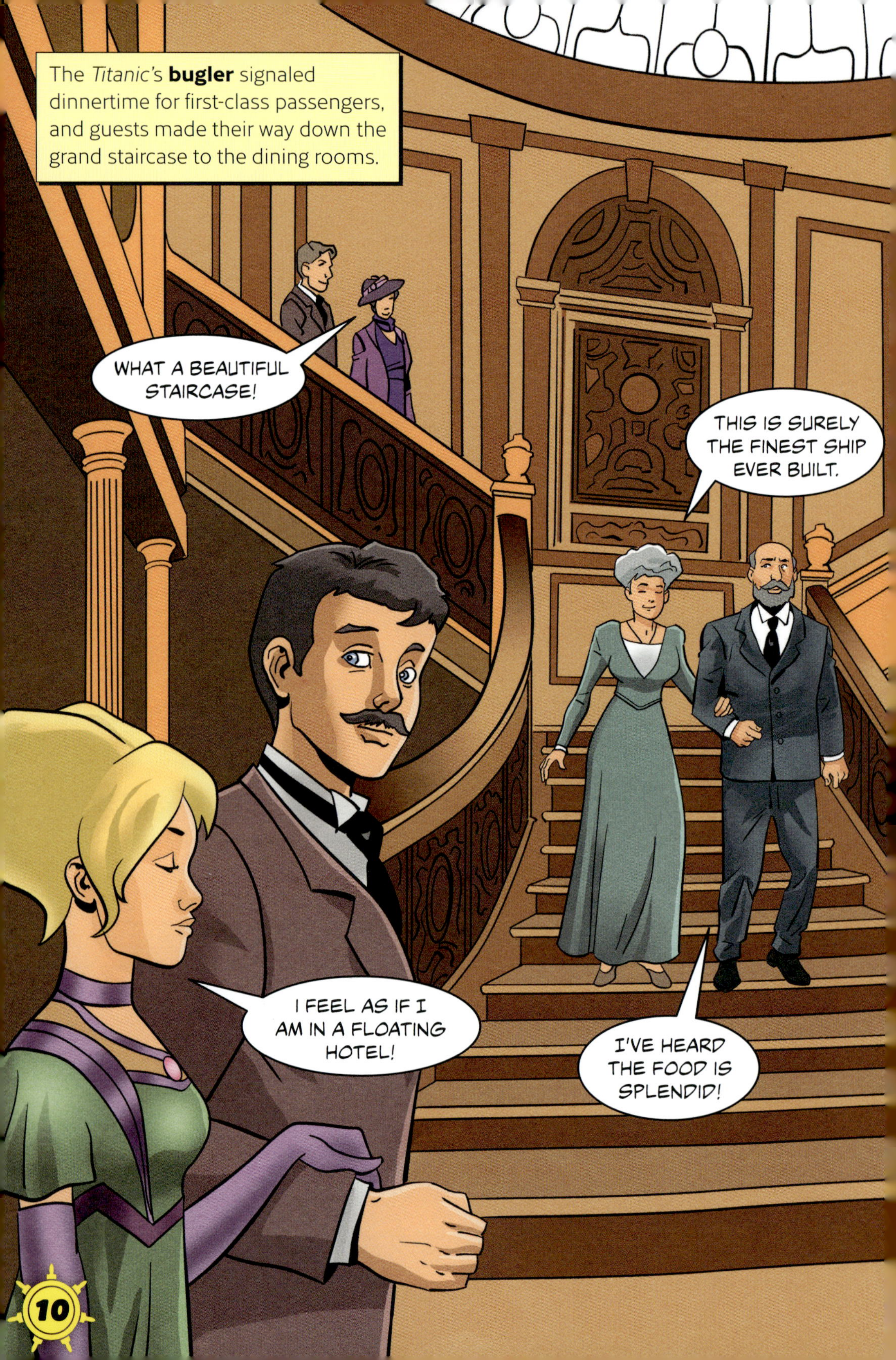
WHAT A BEAUTIFUL STAIRCASE!
THIS IS SURELY THE FINEST SHIP EVER BUILT.
I FEEL AS IF I AM IN A FLOATING HOTEL!
I'VE HEARD THE FOOD IS SPLENDID!

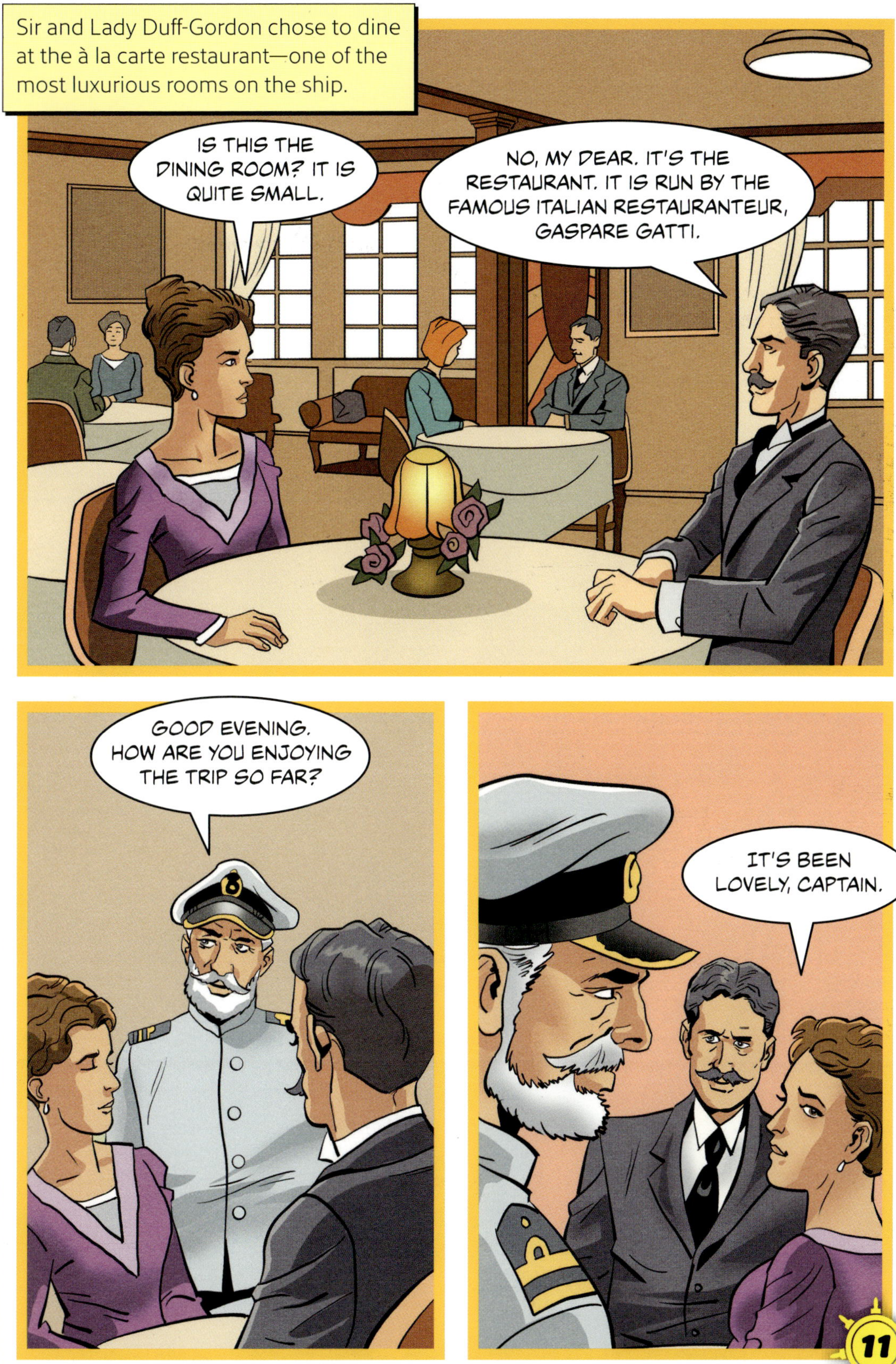
Sir and Lady Duff-Gordon chose to dine at the à la carte restaurant—one of the most luxurious rooms on the ship.
IS THIS THE DINING ROOM? IT IS QUITE SMALL.
NO, MY DEAR. IT'S THE RESTAURANT. IT IS RUN BY THE FAMOUS ITALIAN RESTAURANTEUR, GASPARE GATTI.
GOOD EVENING. HOW ARE YOU ENJOYING THE TRIP SO FAR?
IT'S BEEN LOVELY, CAPTAIN.

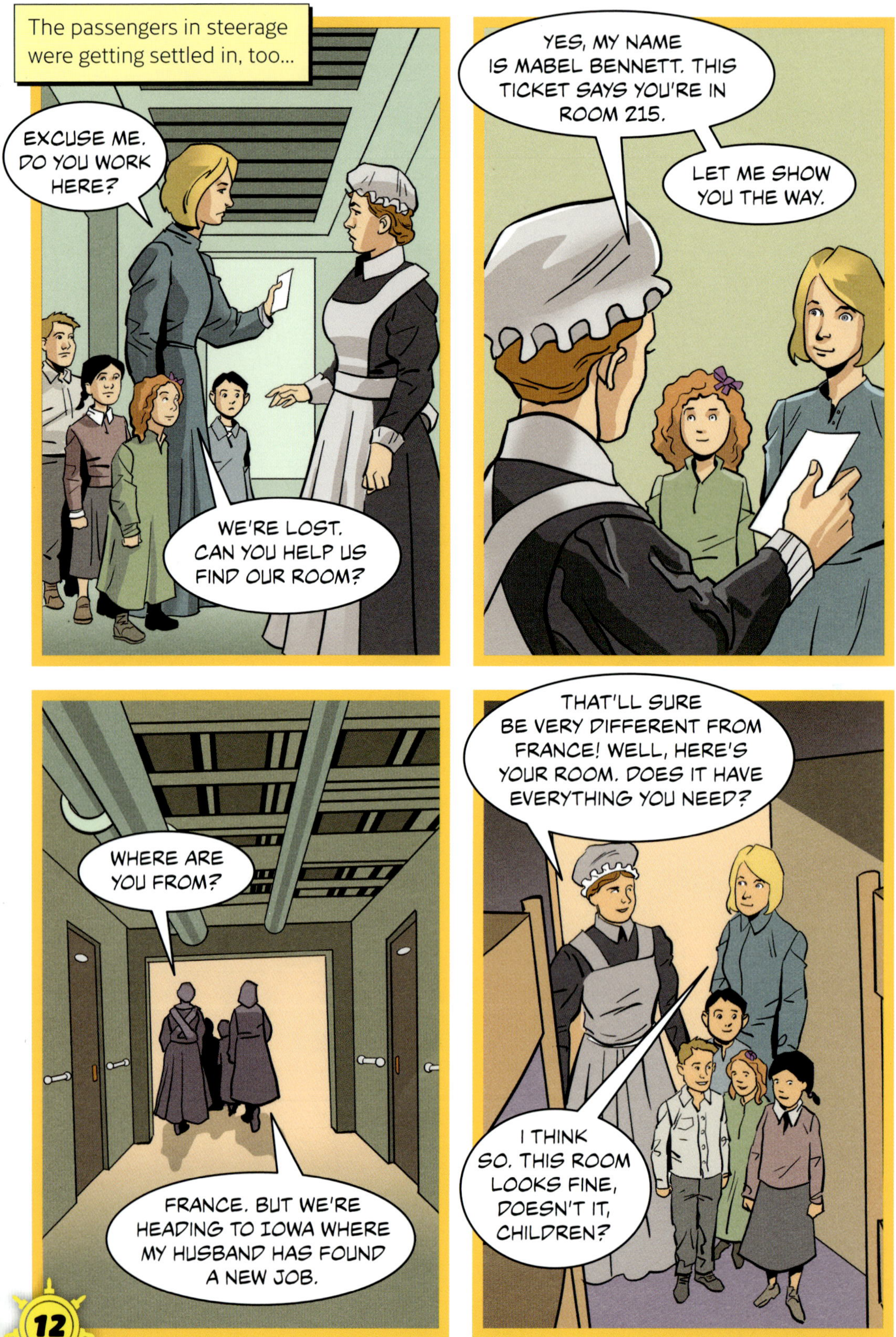
The passengers in steerage were getting settled in, too...
EXCUSE ME. DO YOU WORK HERE?
WE'RE LOST. CAN YOU HELP US FIND OUR ROOM?
YES, MY NAME IS MABEL BENNETT. THIS TICKET SAYS YOU'RE IN ROOM 215.
LET ME SHOW YOU THE WAY.
WHERE ARE YOU FROM?
FRANCE. BUT WE'RE HEADING TO IOWA WHERE MY HUSBAND HAS FOUND A NEW JOB.
THAT'LL SURE BE VERY DIFFERENT FROM FRANCE! WELL, HERE'S YOUR ROOM. DOES IT HAVE EVERYTHING YOU NEED?
I THINK SO. THIS ROOM LOOKS FINE, DOESN'T IT, CHILDREN?

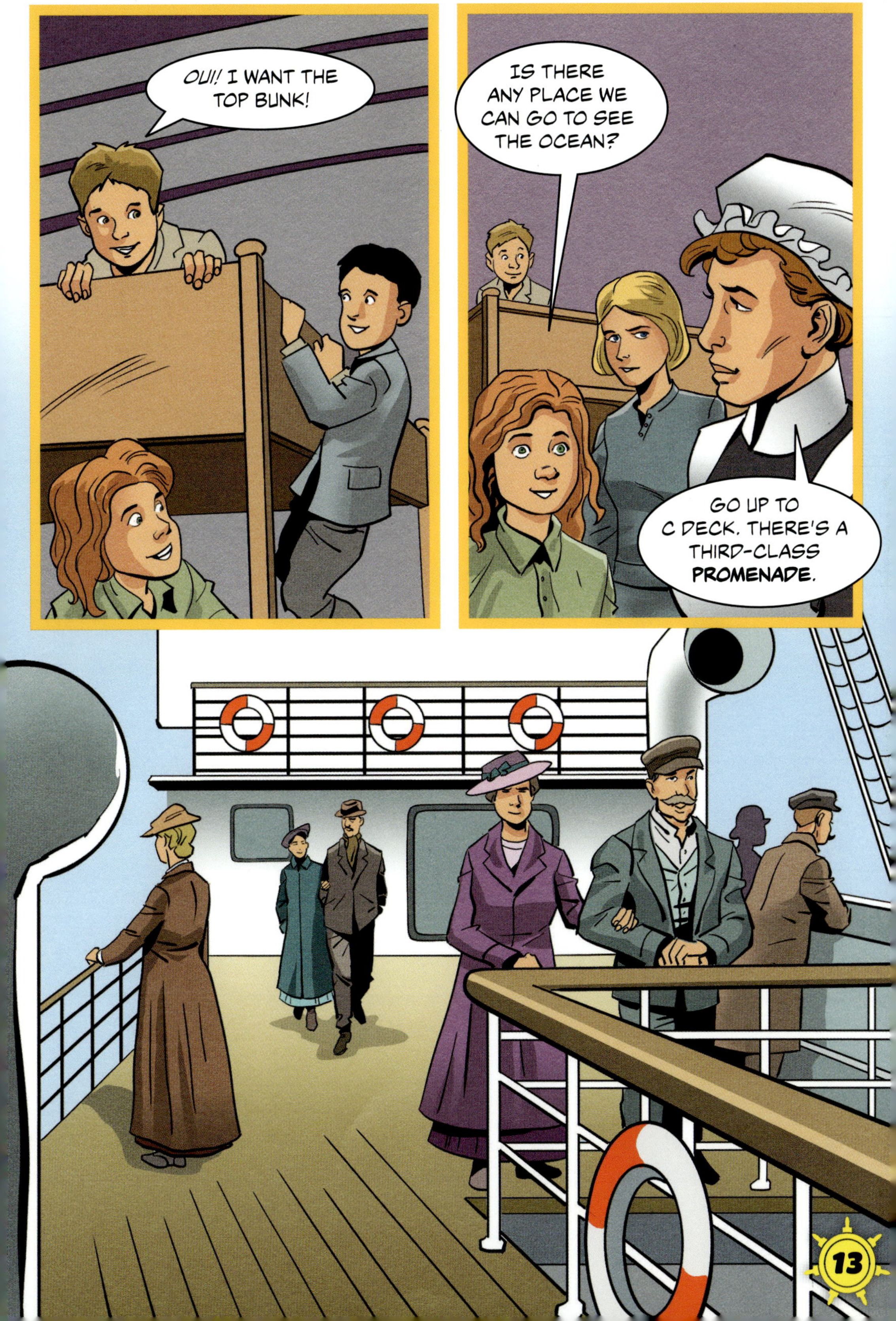

OUI! I WANT THE TOP BUNK!
IS THERE ANY PLACE WE CAN GO TO SEE THE OCEAN?
GO UP TO C DECK. THERE'S A THIRD-CLASS **PROMENADE**.

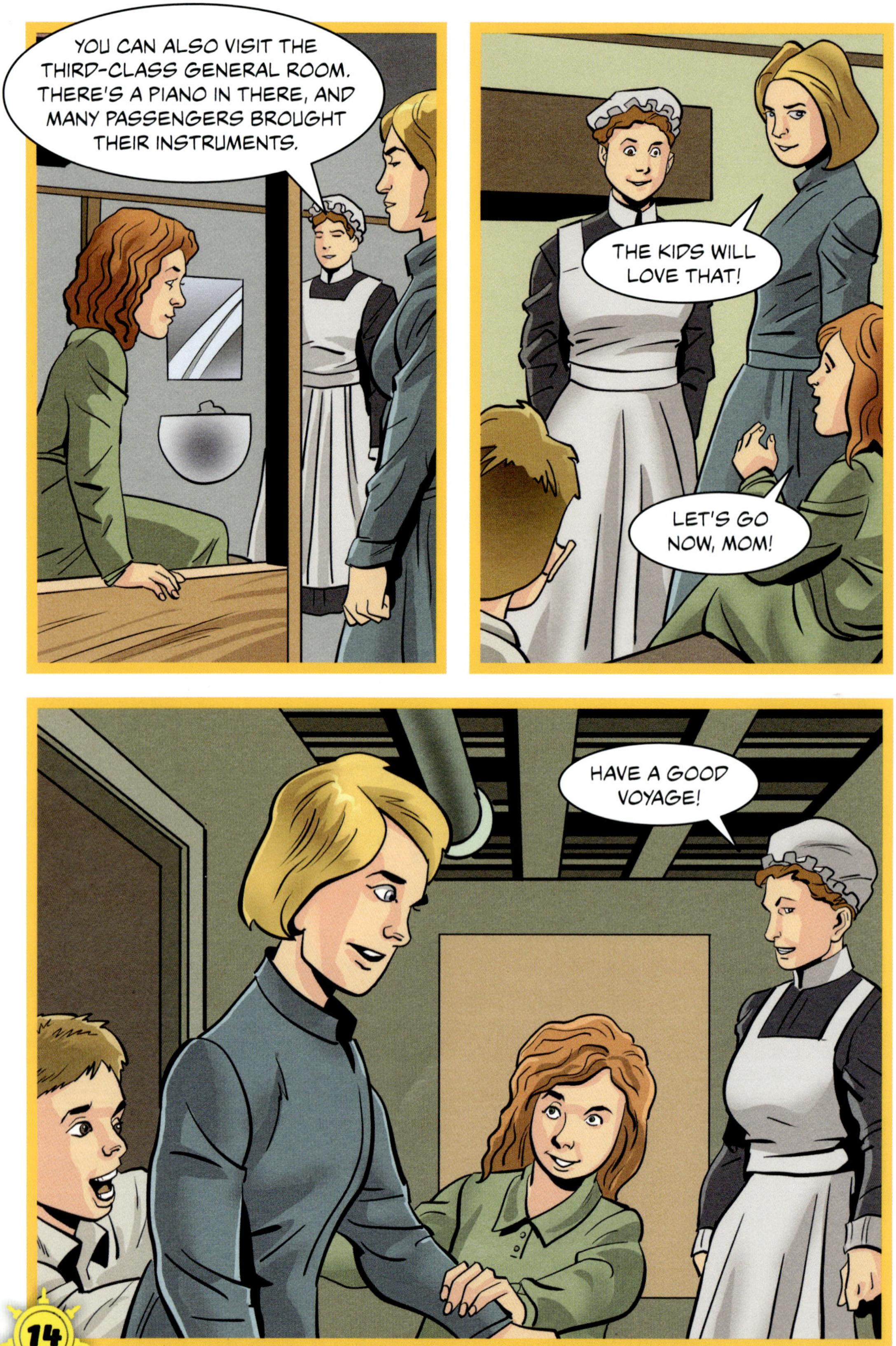
YOU CAN ALSO VISIT THE THIRD-CLASS GENERAL ROOM. THERE'S A PIANO IN THERE, AND MANY PASSENGERS BROUGHT THEIR INSTRUMENTS.
THE KIDS WILL LOVE THAT!
LET'S GO NOW, MOM!
HAVE A GOOD VOYAGE!

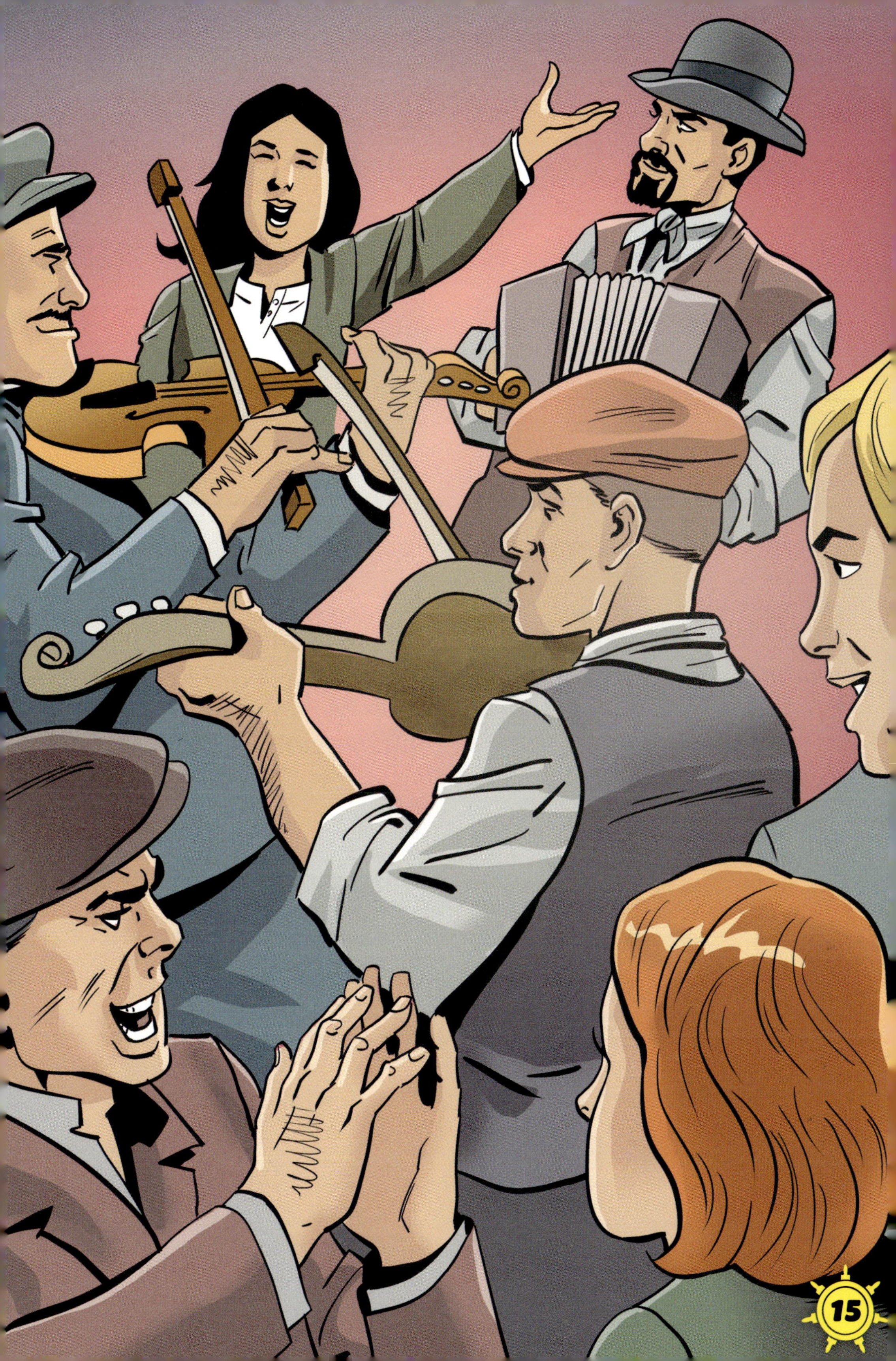

CHAPTER 3

Iceberg, Right Ahead!

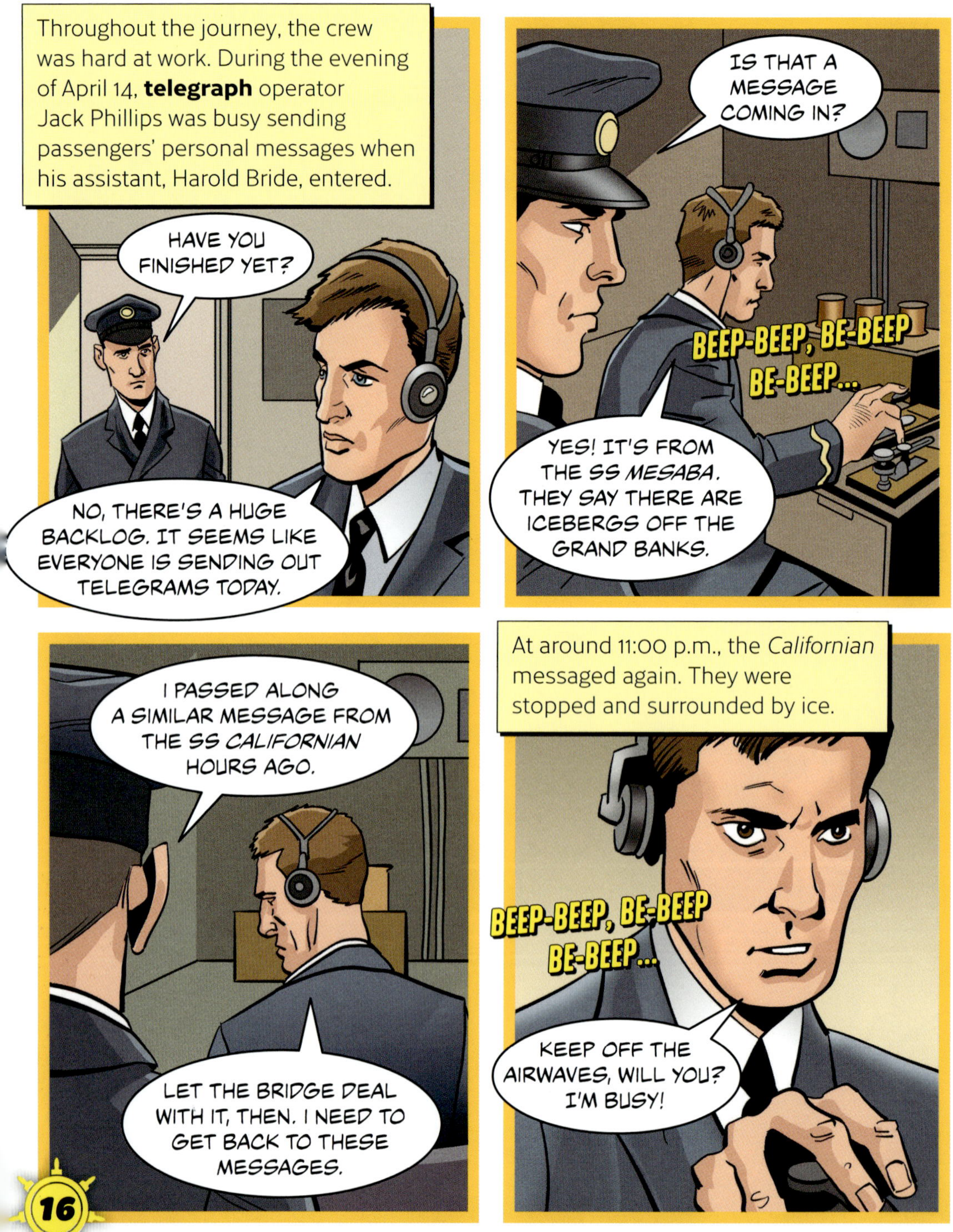
Throughout the journey, the crew was hard at work. During the evening of April 14, **telegraph** operator Jack Phillips was busy sending passengers' personal messages when his assistant, Harold Bride, entered.
HAVE YOU FINISHED YET?
NO, THERE'S A HUGE BACKLOG. IT SEEMS LIKE EVERYONE IS SENDING OUT TELEGRAMS TODAY.
IS THAT A MESSAGE COMING IN?
BEEP-BEEP, BE-BEEP BE-BEEP...
YES! IT'S FROM THE SS *MESABA*. THEY SAY THERE ARE ICEBERGS OFF THE GRAND BANKS.
I PASSED ALONG A SIMILAR MESSAGE FROM THE SS *CALIFORNIAN* HOURS AGO.
LET THE BRIDGE DEAL WITH IT, THEN. I NEED TO GET BACK TO THESE MESSAGES.
At around 11:00 p.m., the *Californian* messaged again. They were stopped and surrounded by ice.
BEEP-BEEP, BE-BEEP BE-BEEP...
KEEP OFF THE AIRWAVES, WILL YOU? I'M BUSY!

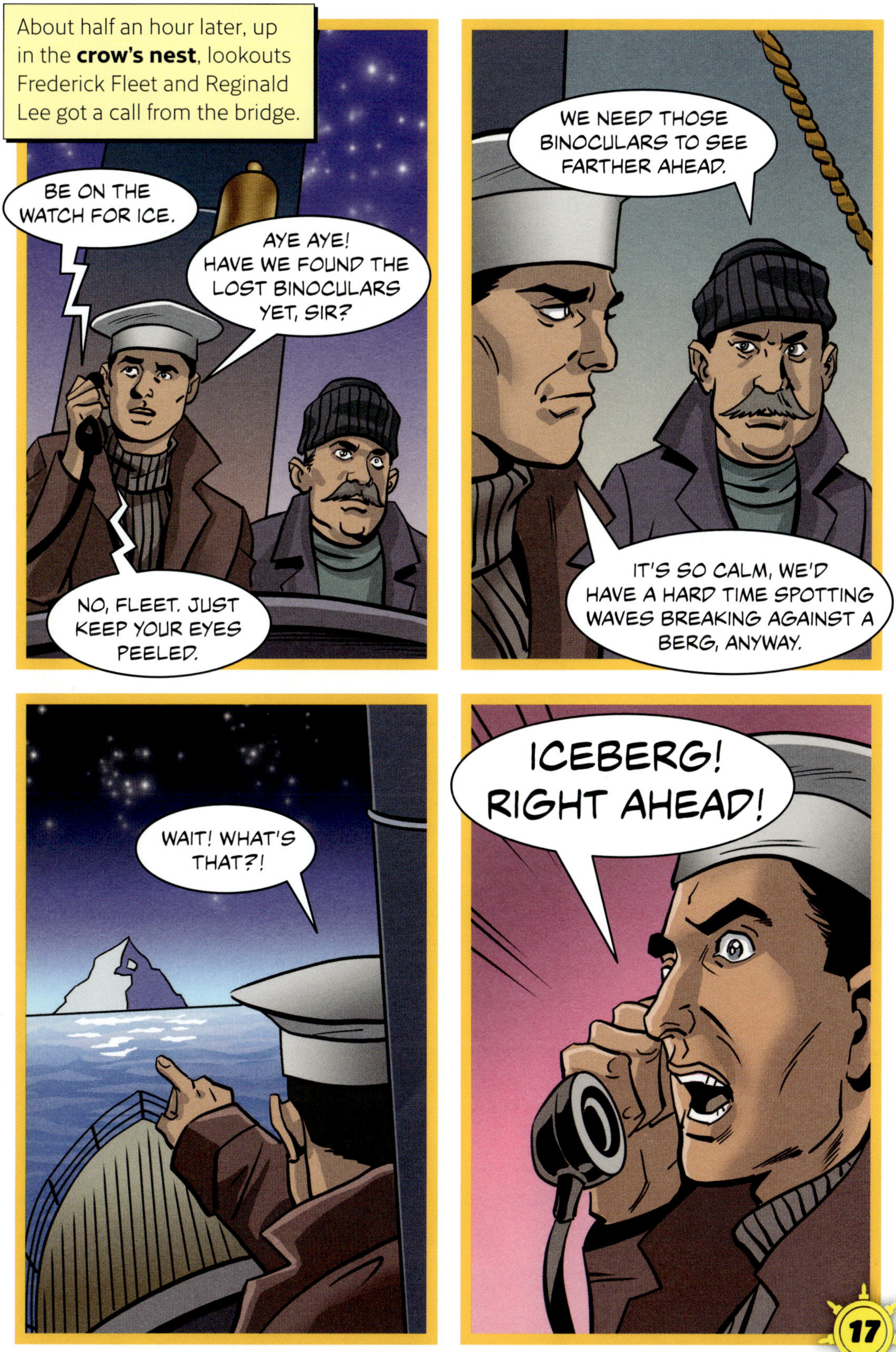
About half an hour later, up in the **crow's nest**, lookouts Frederick Fleet and Reginald Lee got a call from the bridge.
BE ON THE WATCH FOR ICE.
AYE AYE! HAVE WE FOUND THE LOST BINOCULARS YET, SIR?
NO, FLEET. JUST KEEP YOUR EYES PEELED.
WE NEED THOSE BINOCULARS TO SEE FARTHER AHEAD.
IT'S SO CALM, WE'D HAVE A HARD TIME SPOTTING WAVES BREAKING AGAINST A BERG, ANYWAY.
WAIT! WHAT'S THAT?!
ICEBERG! RIGHT AHEAD!

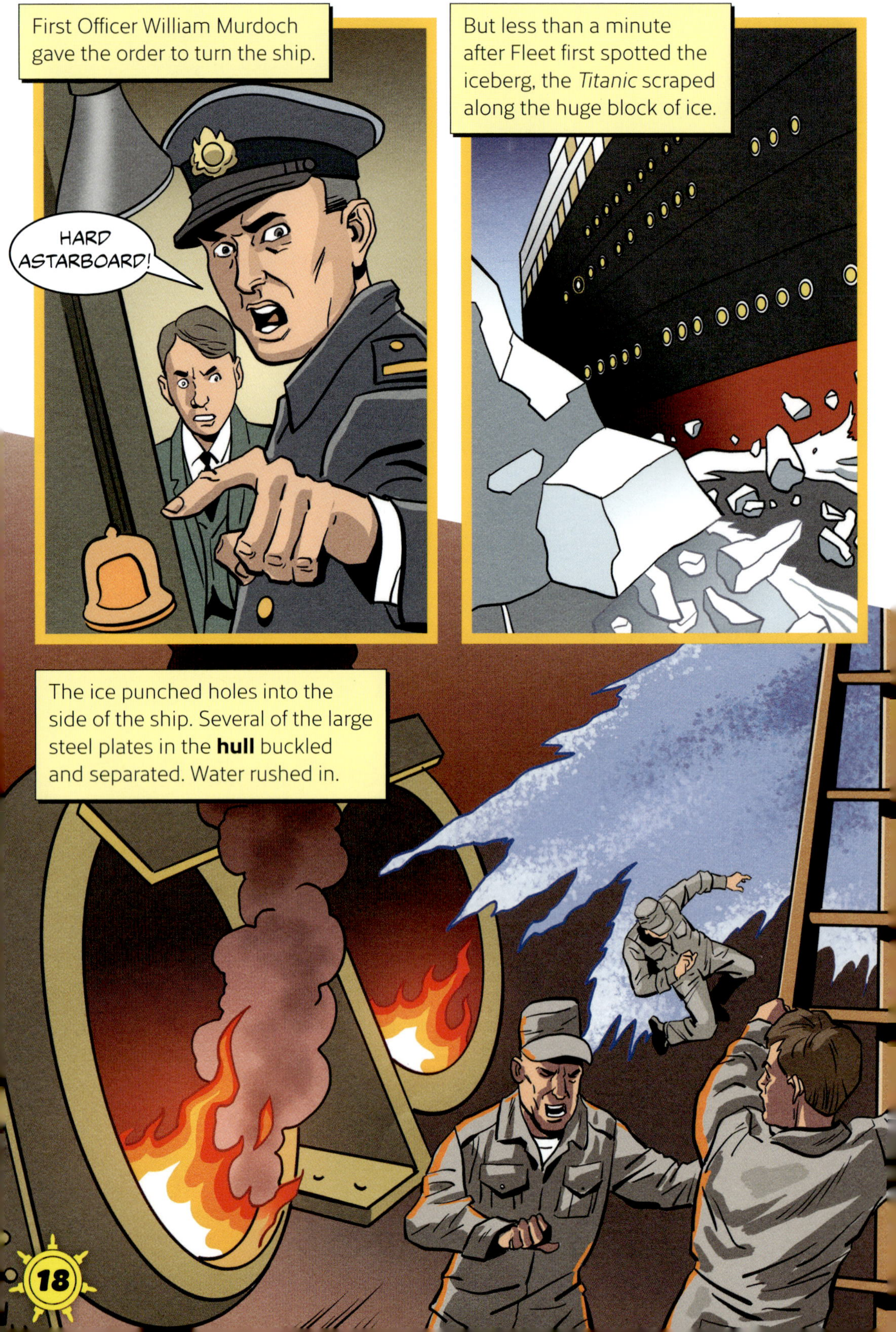
First Officer William Murdoch gave the order to turn the ship.
HARD ASTARBOARD!
But less than a minute after Fleet first spotted the iceberg, the *Titanic* scraped along the huge block of ice.
The ice punched holes into the side of the ship. Several of the large steel plates in the **hull** buckled and separated. Water rushed in.

Titanic was built with 16 watertight compartments. Large doors could be shut to block off any compartments that were flooded. Captain Smith gave orders to do just that.

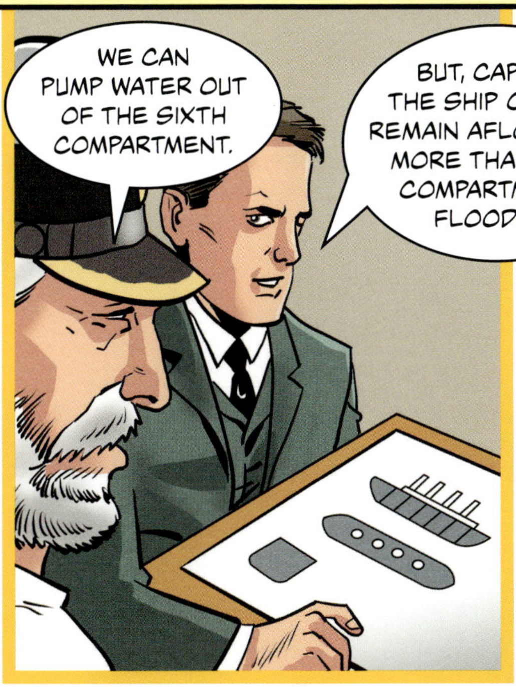
WE CAN PUMP WATER OUT OF THE SIXTH COMPARTMENT.
BUT, CAPTAIN, THE SHIP CANNOT REMAIN AFLOAT WITH MORE THAN FOUR COMPARTMENTS FLOODED!

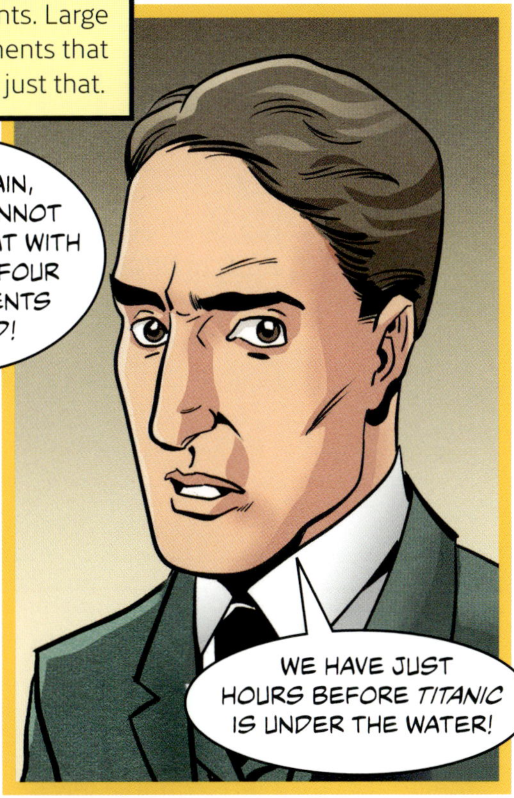
WE HAVE JUST HOURS BEFORE *TITANIC* IS UNDER THE WATER!

Lifeboats were launched and flares were fired into the sky to alert any nearby ships. But for many, help came too late...

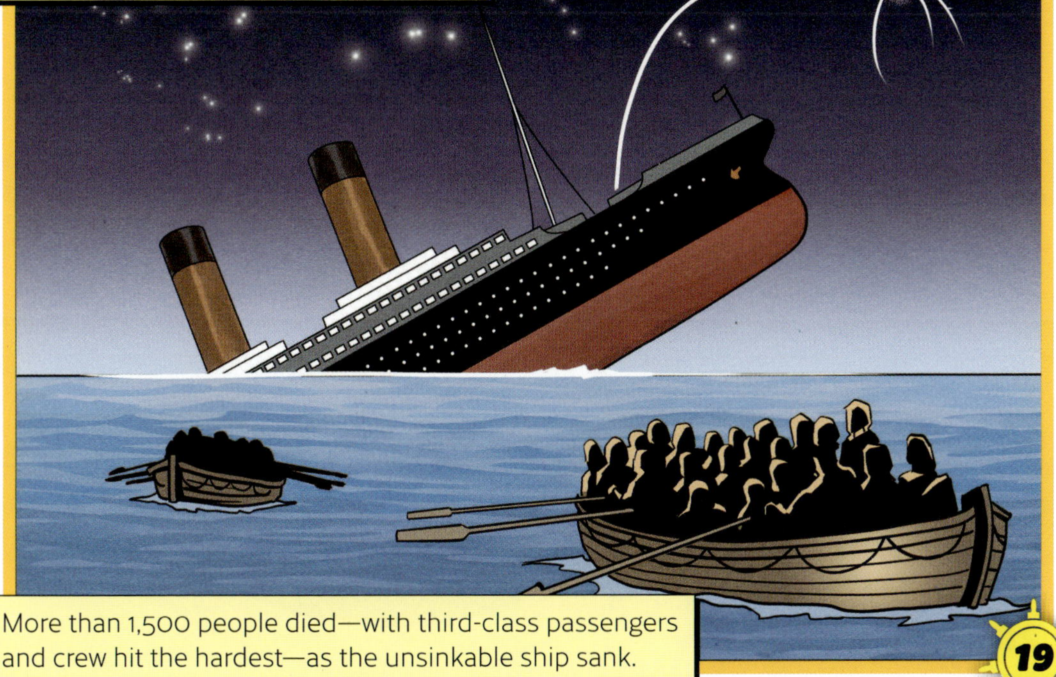

More than 1,500 people died—with third-class passengers and crew hit the hardest—as the unsinkable ship sank.

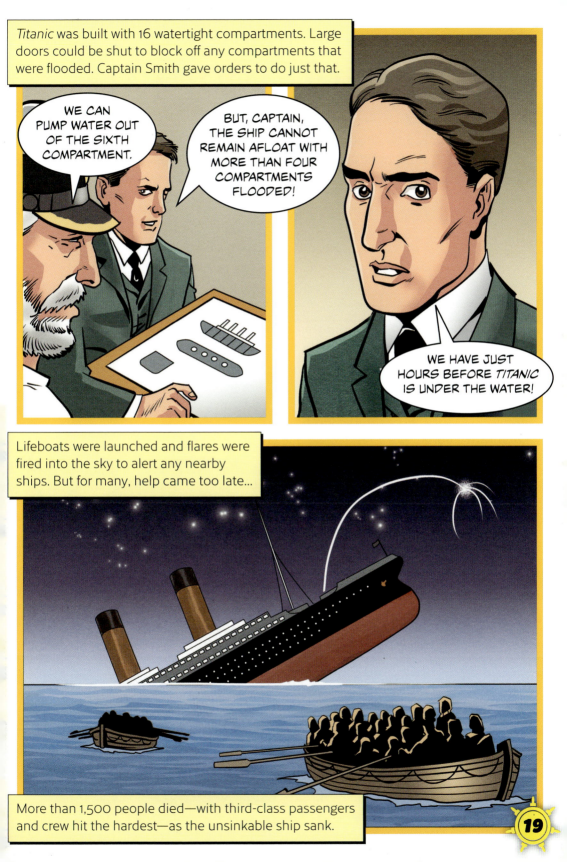

A Deadly Accident

Titanic was built to be strong and sturdy. The base of the ship was divided into 16 watertight compartments that could be sealed off. In the event of a collision, doors between the compartments would close, keeping any water from spreading. Originally, the walls, called bulkheads, between these compartments were designed to reach the higher decks, but they were ultimately shortened to give the first-class dining hall more space.

On the night of the accident, *Titanic* was traveling at almost full speed when crew members spotted an iceberg. Despite efforts to steer away, the right front side of the ship scraped against the ice. This left gashes in the hull of the boat, popping rivets and buckling plates. Water rushed in, flooding two compartments and quickly filling four more. Although the crew shut the doors, the bulkheads were too short. Water flowed over the top. Soon, water began to weigh down the front of the ship. Within a few hours, *Titanic* had sunk.

A REPLICA OF ONE OF *TITANIC'S* WATERTIGHT DOORS

As the ship went down, passengers began to board lifeboats. Unfortunately, the chaos of the night meant some boats were launched before they were full. There were also not enough lifeboats on board to save everyone traveling on the *Titanic*. Many lives were lost.

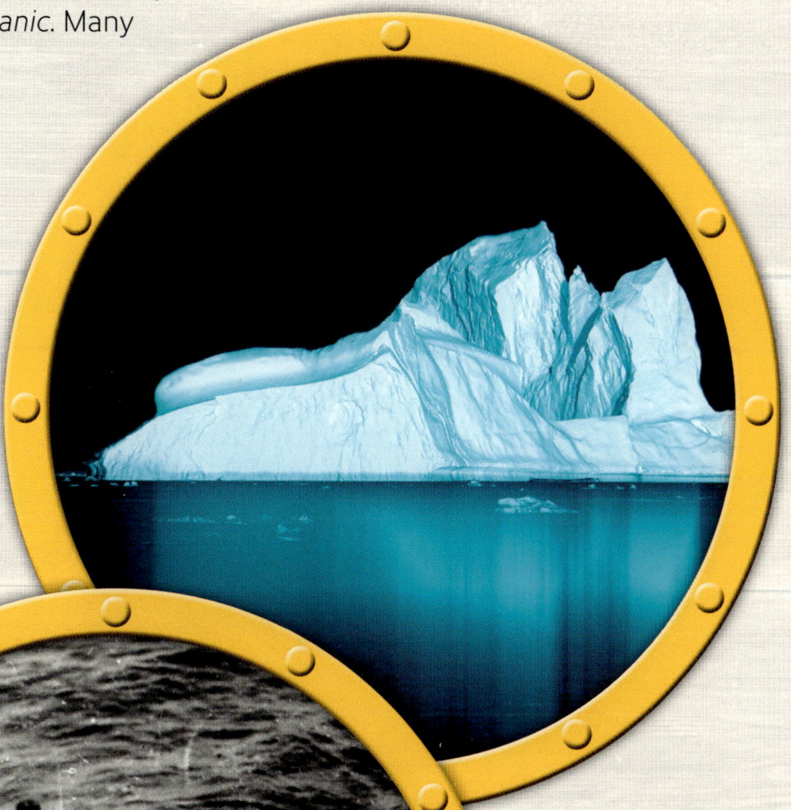

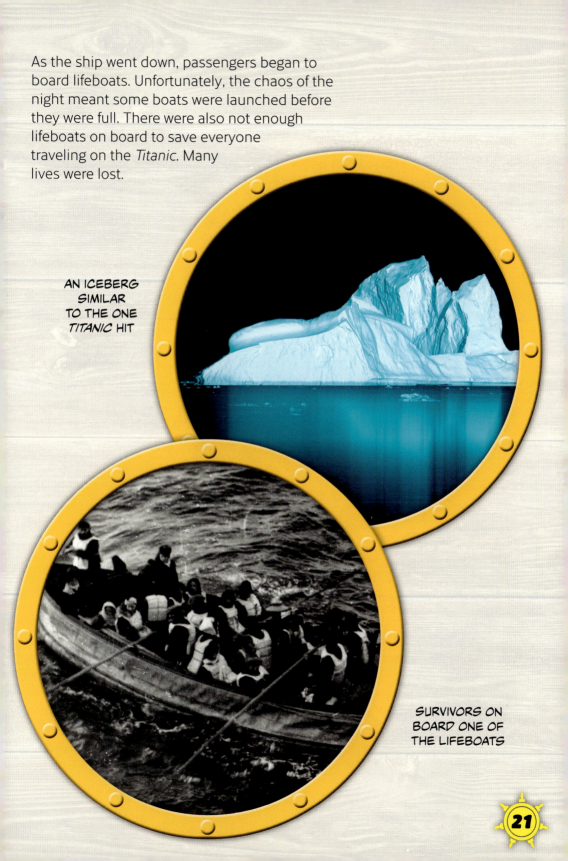

AN ICEBERG SIMILAR TO THE ONE *TITANIC* HIT

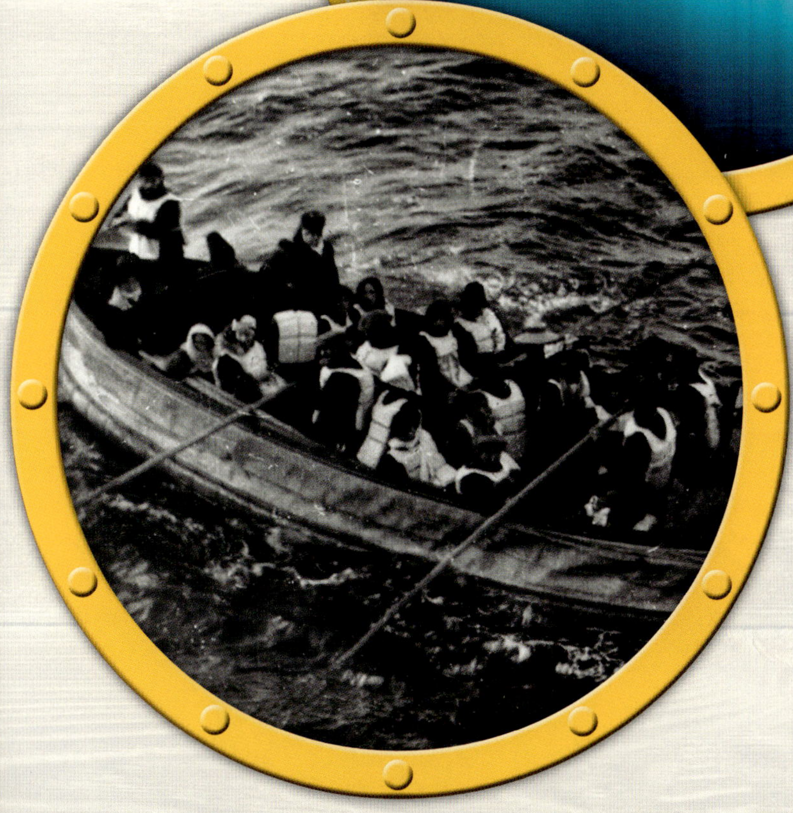

SURVIVORS ON BOARD ONE OF THE LIFEBOATS

More Titanic Stories

Frederick Fleet was on watch in the crow's nest the night the *Titanic* went under. It was difficult to see in the darkness, and the binoculars he would typically use had been misplaced. Making things even harder, there were no waves breaking in the calm waters. When he finally spotted the iceberg, it was too close, and the ship was traveling too fast. In the evacuation that followed, Fleet helped women and children board a lifeboat, before joining. The boat was rowed to safety. Fleet and these passengers were rescued by RMS *Carpathia* four hours after *Titanic* sunk.

FREDERICK FLEET

CAPTAIN EDWARD SMITH

Captain Smith had worked at sea for more than 40 years. Upon hearing of ice in the water, he changed *Titanic*'s course slightly, but he didn't reduce the ship's speed. He thought there would be plenty of time to avoid any potential collisions. Smith was in his cabin when the iceberg struck but immediately came on deck. When he learned of the ship's fate, he gave orders to alert passengers and to uncover the lifeboats. He had his crew send out distress calls and fire signal rockets. He did everything he could. Smith went down with the ship. His body was never found.

Glossary

accelerate to change speed, often used to mean going faster

amenities things that provide comfort, convenience, or enjoyment

astern toward the rear of a ship

bugler someone who plays a brass instrument called a bugle

crow's nest a high platform on a ship, used as a place to keep watch

equipment items that are used for a particular purpose

hull the main body of a ship, including the bottom, sides, and deck

liner a large, luxurious passenger ship

promenade an area on the deck of a ship where passengers can walk

route the course taken to get to a destination

telegraph a system for sending long-distance messages, called telegrams

Index

Read More

Kerry, Isaac. *Inside the* Titanic *(Top Secret).* Minneapolis: Lerner Publications, 2023.

Long, David. *Tragedy at Sea: The Sinking of the* Titanic. New York: Union Square Kids, 2024.

Son, John. *Aboard the* Titanic *(A True Book).* New York: Scholastic Inc., 2022.

Learn More Online

1. Go to **FactSurfer.com** or scan the QR code below.
2. Enter "**Deadly Journey**" into the search box.
3. Click on the cover of this book to see a list of websites.